The
Value
System
of
Leadership

Wisdom K. Ogbuagu

The Value System of leadership

All scripture quotations are from the king James version of the Bible, except otherwise stated.

A key for other Bible translation used:

NKJV   New Kings James Version

GNB   Good News Bible

RSV   Revised Standard Version

NIV   New International Version

TANT   The Amplified New Translation

AMP   The Amplified Bible

NRSV   New Revised Standard Version

First Published by Chiysonovelty International 2016

ISBN: 9785317676
ISBN-13: 978-9785317671

Chiysonovelty International

Plot 8 Evule Avenue

Aba,

Nigeria

Email: chiyson@minister.com

Phone: 234-909-227-1088

Printed in the United States of America

To God Be the Glory, Great Things He has done.

DEDICATION

To God Almighty for the enablement To the human hearts. To all individuals who have found life to be a mere shadow of their personality, who think they are here to make up the numbers in their organization and who are aimless, busy but not effective in their personal lives.

To you the reader, for whom I desire a fulfilled, purposeful, efficient, and effective destiny to enable you to pursue your career with definite understanding of what leadership is all about, and the right approach to it.

To all who are oppressed by the ignorance of what leadership are all about and what a leader stands for. To everyone that sincerely seeks to give his career and organization a meaning for existence. To everyone who is seeking to know the nitty-gritty of leadership and grow in all round knowledge.

"When leadership misses the complex values of leadership they are mostly likely bound to make a shipwreck of the system and when the system is having challenges, the leadership might be missing in one of the value system that makes leadership work." - Wisdom K. Ogbuagu

CONTENTS

ACKNOWLEDGMENTS

We are the sum total of what we have learnt from all who have taught us either by books, CDs, tapes, etc. I am eternally grateful to all mentors that have nurtured me in one way or the other, both great and small, death or alive. They truly left me with the roots of unending sources of wisdom.

To all members and friends of and colleagues in Wiskele Nets Limited, I am grateful. I am also grateful to those whose faithfulness, courage, patience and, prayers have inspired me to continue to fulfill God's given potentials and gifts. Thank you all for standing by me.

For the development of this book, I feel a great sense of gratitude to: To my mother, Mrs. Grace Ogbuagu, Mama, you made it easier for me to fulfill the divine purpose for my life and career. I will always love you.

My father, late Mr. Johnson Ogbuagu, who believed in me when others found it difficult to truly believe in me. Dad, you always told me that I would end up great. You implanted the seed of greatness when I was still small. Thank you for your great support. I love you.

My mentors, whom I have learnt so much from, and it is from all I have been taught from each and every one of you that gave birth to this book, I am proud to be associated with every one of you through books; my spiritual father Bishop David Oyedepo,

Kenneth and Gloria Copeland, Late Kenneth E. Hagen, Papa Enoch Adeboye, Pastor Matthew Ashimolowo, John C. Maxwell, Bishop Benson Edahosa, Dr. Myles Munroe, Smith Wigglesworth Rev. Dr. Uma Ukpai, T. L. Osborn.

Pastor Nwagu Okenwa you are my pastor, friend, counselor, and teacher. You have imparted so much to my destiny. Even though you spend little time in my life, it is still effective. Pastor Emeka Chris David, I love. You scold me as leader, play with me as a friend, and encourage me as a brother, thank you for being there for me. Uncle Chris Harry thanks for your all-round support and many more I can't remember; God bless each an every one of you.

My friends, John Oboh, Samuel Okechukwu, thanks for your honest encouragement to this work. Gospel Okorie, my personal assistance and secretary of our organization, you are my colleague who became a dear friend. I want to especially and sincerely thank you for your all-round support to see to the success of this book, and for your incredible service and willingness to go the extra mile every day.

My proof reader Dr. Joseph Adiorho you have done wonderfully well in editing my works. Without your contribution, this book would have been a mess. I am eternally grateful to God for bringing people like you around my destiny.

INTRODUCTION

Every great organization has a great system that sustains the value of the organization, business, and cooperation. Organization that must stand the test of time must operate by system and that is what brings out the beauty and the growth of such a sector.

A system is a combination of related parts organized into a complex whole. It is also a scheme of ideas or principles by which something is organized. Example, the democratic system, Friend hear this; the value the leadership placed on the system is what determined the value your followers will place on the organization. When leadership lacks value it naturally lacks followership and when the place of value is misplaced the place of system is misunderstood.

Value system of leadership is all about understanding the system and the value leadership carries and to get a clear view of the system in leadership. Friend understand this, every system has a value attached to it and when a court clear value is missing the leader is bound to have challenges with the system. Virtually everything in the world today operate by system, for you to fly you must follow instructed systems same with swimming, driving, eating, etc. you can't say because am tired of trekking let me use my hand and do the trekking no, it doesn't work that way same in leadership it is govern by complex principles that makes it work any of the principles you miss you would have miss something vital in your leadership. It might interest you to note, every field works by principles until you work by those principles you cannot become a principality in that field. Friend, you need the principles to rule. Let's look at what leadership is in this contest.

LEADERSHIP

- is influence generated by passion motivated by vision produce by purpose achieved by values placed on the system.
- is a product of influence generated by value placed on the system.
- is ability to influence through the complexity of values that makes the system works.

When leadership misses the complex values of leadership they are mostly likely bound to make a shipwreck of the system and when the system is having challenges, the leadership might be missing in one of the value system that makes leadership work.

In my continent Africa some of the leaders in quote are making a shipwreck of the value system in leadership, this is where somebody will want to rule a nation as if he is ruling his house keepers. A place where somebody will be in power for more then thirty years without thinking of handing over power, where the value system of leadership has been reduced to it's zero level without respect for the rule of law, where a positional leader thinks he is above the law in fact he is the law himself. Friend, the true test of leadership is in it power. Your true value will be tested when you occupy a position of authority. That is while I want to x-ray leadership through the value system it contains and carries.

I will really appreciate you, take your take to read through the contents of this masterpiece and be inspired to excel in your individual field of endeavors as you pursue your dreams, vision, desires, and goals.

Have a great time with this work of a genius.

CHAPTER ONE

VISIONARY LEADERSHIP

Though, in the midst of the bad and heartless rulers there are men and women in Africa that is making distinguishing contribution in the world and Africa to see to the development of their people despite the ups and down, circumstances that surrounds them and the thick Cloud of discouragement that come their way . Friend, the best of visionary leaders is seen when the leader is surrounded by a thick cloud of discouragements and misfortune are so glaring before him. That is the case of this African leader, the late president of Malawi Bingu Wa Mutharika.

REVOLUTIONIZE AGRICULTURAL SECTOR

Between 2002 and 2006 this African country experience extreme food shortage which was coursed by indescribable rains and flood. Between 2007 and 2008 Malawians had so much food in the stock not only to feed themselves but to give to their neighboring country not only did they give food but become advisers in agriculture to their neighboring country.

THE MAGIC

President Bingu Wa Mutharika took charge of agricultural sector when he came into office. The government under him implemented sustainable policy program on agricultural subsidy but this man did not just state the policy program he rolled it with a clear vision, friend it might interest you to note, visionary leaders see it, say it, go for it, and achieves it. He wanted to see the down trodden, lack, famine Malawian feed themselves again, this man knew it is possible considering the land and fresh waters, Malawians definitely could.

The government started with small scale farmers by giving them new superior crop breeds, fertilizers, irrigation system and educate them on crop rotation and soil management. They empowered their farmers through education that made them became aware of their environments and climatic condition of their nation. Visionary leadership is the ability to take a vision from the basic to the needful; that was the case of Bingu Wa Muttharika, he succeeds from taking that vision away from him and making it a country vision. John W. Gardner said "the prospects never looked brighter and the problems never looked tougher. Anyone who isn't stirred by both of those statements is too tired to be of much use to us in the days ahead". With the irrigation the farmers worry some state and massive rainfall became a thing of the past. And with Agro-science the government was able to fight and stop poor agricultural methods.

This where done through National program implemented with fund from AGRA where local shopkeepers got grants to subsidize fertilizer and hybrid seeds as well as training. They had opportunity to advise farmers on what to use, when and where to use them. The farmers in Malawi moved from 800 kg to 2500 kg per hectare production of maize three times their usual production. Food shortage became a thing of the past in Malawi they could feed themselves and have surplus to give out, food was running over government silos. Today this man is a celebrity in his country Malawi.

This story is an indication that the original perception of the outside world about Africa and African continents can't feed themselves is obviously not true but the challenges lies within us like president Bingu Wa Mutharika will always say "*Africa is not poor but Africans are poor*" this man has shown what visionary leadership and what he has done for his own country that is his own legacy. When we speak of Malawi today is not about drought but about food sustenance Bingu boosted "*Malawi cannot be poor, let alone beg food, with all the fertile land and fresh waters stretching across the whole country. Never.*"₁

Friend, visionary leaders are the builder of new world, working with the power of imagination, insight, hindsight, and boldness. They go beyond conceiving a vision but they conceive and bring it into reality with all power within them. They see the picture, with their inner eyes and

ഇൽ

Visionary leaders are the builder of new world, working with the power of imagination, insight, hindsight, and boldness.

ഇൽ

bring it to reality and the world around them to see it with their physical eyes. They are innovators and world changers; they know how to use the elemental forces of change to bring about a new world to their world that is what distinguishes them from ordinary visionaries. What adds value to a visionary leader is his ability to go beyond his length and breadth of his vision to add value to his people that is when the vision becomes more beneficial to his people or followers more then his selfish interest this course absolute influence to leadership. No leader fully enjoys influence positively when he lacks the qualities of influence as describe by John C. Maxwell in his book *"360 degree leader."*

INTEGRITY	*Building relationship on trust*
NURTURING	*Cares about people as individuals*
FAITH	*Believes in people*
LISTENING	*Values what others have to say*
UNDERSTANDING	*Sees from their point of view*
ENLARGING	*Helps others become bigger*
NAVIGATING	*Assists others through difficulties*
CONNECTING	*Initiates positives relationships*
EMPOWERING	*Gives them the power to lead$_2$*

INSPIRATIONAL VISION

Every successful visionary leadership in any industry of life today carries with it an inspirational vision. A clear sense of direction that is, how to get their "without vision (*direction*) the people perish (*proverb*), a positive picture of the future (Jeremiah 1:5) "before I formed thee I know thee. A visionless leader is a leader who does not have goals, dreams, inspirations, and the will power to fulfill destiny. Friends hear this; vision is what brings energy into form. When energy is lacking vision might be missing. Nelson Mandela held his positive vision to abolish apartheid in south Africa despite the challenges from the government of South Africa then, he could not stop because the will power and what sustains energy which is vision was there. This visionary leader saw beyond what his natural eye could see, and it might interest you to note, visionary leaders see with their mind and look with their eye. What he saw sustained him in the prison yard for 27 years and hear this, it is not who fought you that matters it is the dream you carry that matters. Late Nelson became a leaving legend in this present world.

Vision is what brings energy into form. When energy is lacking vision might be missing.

Every true inspirational vision brings about an aspirational revolution also every lack of inspirational vision brings with it expiration in any venture or organisation.

Visionary leader transmits a sound communication by themselves by representing their vision, as the author Margaret Wheatley notes *"they keep communicating to create a strong field which then brings their vision into physical reality"* that was the case of another legend in Asia and the world today his name is Mahatma Gandhi. He was highly committed to his religion and his people, this man became the leader of nonviolent movement to free Indians he was known as the Mahatma which mean the great soul. He fought for the peace between Hindus and Muslims throughout his country. This great visionary leader is known in the world today as a symbol of nonviolence, his diplomacy and strategy were later adopted and used by this great African America Martin Luther King Jr. To gain equality for his peoples the African Americans.

Visionary leaders inspire their followers to be effective and better then they already are and he then discovers what Abraham Lincoln called "the angle of their better nature" it was this same power that inspire Martin Luther King Jr. *"I have a dream"* speech. Every true inspirational vision brings about an aspirational revolution also every lack of inspirational vision brings with it expiration in any venture or organization. Friend hear this, every vision most be filtered through the carrier of the vision, the truth still remains that your followers buy into you before they buy into your vision.

Visionary leadership is not a title it is ability to see it and achieved it. It might interest you to note, the leader finds the vision and then the followers and the followers finds the leader and then the vision. What makes Mohandas K. Gandhi popularly known as Mahatma Gandhi known in the world is not just because he used nonviolence to achieve freedom but his ability to impart his vision of nonviolence to his people through inspiration. Before this time his people has been using violence to have their freedom but to Gandhi it was a different ball game his style was nonviolence and civil disobedience. He once said *"nonviolence is the greatest force at disposal of mankind. It is mightier then the mightiest weapon of destruction devised by the ingenuity of men."*

1919 at Amritsar when the British military massacred more then one thousand people Gandhi called his people to stay calm they obeyed him, he called for everyone to burn foreign made clothe and start wearing nothing but homespun material millions of people in Indian obeyed him he decides that a march to the sea to protest the salt act would be their rallying point for civil disobedience against the British they obeyed him and follow him to two hundred miles to the city of Dandy, where they were arrested by representatives of British government.

Though, the process was slow and painful but his vision was strong enough to deliver on 1947 Indians gained home rule. This is how inspirational vision works they bought into him before buying into his vision, friend hear this; you can only influence your followers when your vision has influenced you adequately.

It might interest you to note, the leader finds the vision and then the followers and the followers finds the leader and then the vision

As exemplified by Gandhi he said "I must first be the change I want to see in my world."

VISIONARY LEADERS DON'T PUT THE VISION FIRST

Great leaders understand the importance of the vision very well more then their followers that is while they first of all make their followers believe in them before believing the vision. Every vision is a true reflection of the carrier. People most times don't want to know how valuable the vision is until they know how valuable the carrier of the vision is, friend hear this, people don't go for a viable vision they go for a viable leader who carriers a viable vision. Looking at this diagram describes it very well.

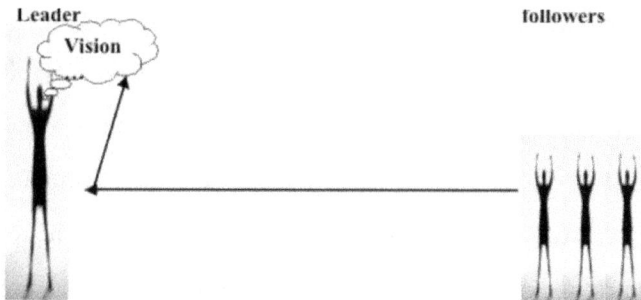

Followers see the leader first before the vision

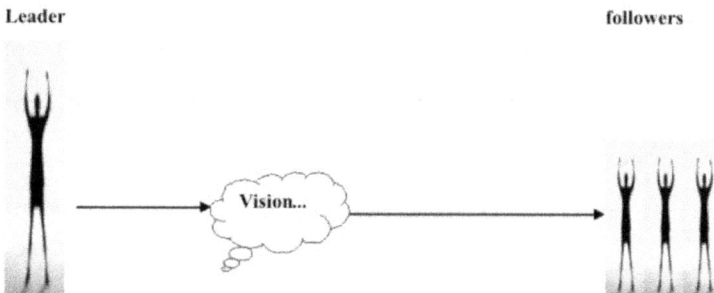

While the leader sees the vision before seeing the followers

The followers align themselves with the vision of the leadership of the organization not the organization to align itself with the vision of the followers look at the next diagram below.

Leader   followers

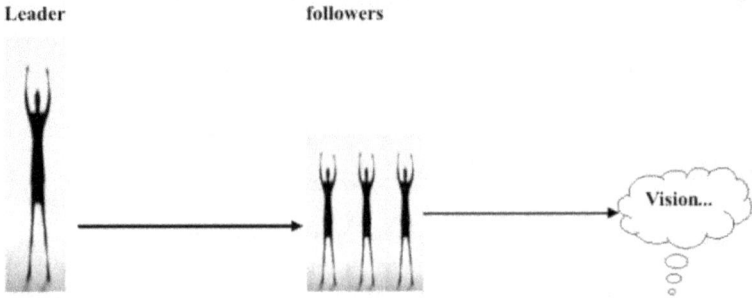

I had this challenge in our organization when we were starting. We were in different things at the same time I hired friends to work in the organization I found it difficult to define each person individual role and could not come out with a sure concrete vision to sustained them and the organization after a while the firm started having challenges nature naturally abhor vacuum, when leadership lacks a vision that align to the destination of the followers the followers create a vision that is inline to their own destination not that of the organization most times.

Friend, hear this, you don't hire somebody you can't fire is very important you note this some are having challenges not because the vision is not good nor the carrier of the vision but because they hire people they can't fire examples friends, cousins, brothers, sisters, fathers etc. I am not saying they are not good they could be good but most times they tend to give the system of the organization nonchalant attitude. What is system?

SAVE YOURSELF TIME, ENERGY AND MONEY

When they give this casual behavior they are actually spending time, energy and money of the organization my advice is, if you cannot fire them don't hire. I learnt my lessons lavishing more than $10,000

VISIONARY LEADERS LEAD BY EXAMPLES

You will believe with me that children learn more by what they see then what they are taught, I remember as a child my parents taught me some valuable moral lessons of life of which if I abide by all I was taught I would have been a role model to my peer group then. When I was growing up I was a very care free person, nothing means anything to me. I always misplace my pen at school and other stuffs. Dad, buys new pen every day along the line he became tired of buying and diverse a method and the method is, anytime I misplace my pen I always will be stricken with a cane which is almost a normal way of correcting a child from this part of the world Africa. He continued beating me with cane I also diverse my own means because am becoming tired of being beaten with a cane, any pen I misplace I will look for another person pen that looks exactly like that my own I will steal it, but back then in school we have a baptismal name for stealing which is called tapping, for one week dad discovered that am always with my pen his mind told him I have been stealing my class mates pen or maybe I have change but I must demystify this change he said. He took my pen and gave it a mark which I didn't know. The upper week I went to school and misplaced that one in my usual way I tap another pen that evening, dad came back and asked me to bring my bag for my homework I cheerfully brought my bag, dad opened my bag and brought out my books and the pen, he looked at the pen with keen interest he didn't see the mark he asked me "who owns this pen?" I said "it is my own" he asked again like three times, I noticed the tune of his voice and face has changed I kept calm I couldn't talk again. He started scolding me "I taught you not to lie but you refused am going to cane you today" I started apologizing to him "dad I will not do it again am sorry please forgive me" crying, suddenly, there was a knock at the door dad peep through the eyes of the door and saw a man inside the house and told me to tell the man he is not around I immediately responded "but dad you are lying" he shouted at me "shut up and do what I said" loll! Friend hear this; leadership is more caught then taught.   Also when you lead by example you become a sample too simple to locate

I have come to realized in life that nothing is more embarrassing and perplexing to a person who give a worthy advice but set unworthy example and friends' putting it the other way round, nothing is more rewarding to a person who give admirable advice and set admirable example.

Peace award winner Albert Schweitzer observed *"example is leadership"* visionary leaders understand that living with what they teach both in words and in character is the most important thing that makes them important in their followers

John wooden is still a legendary UCLA basketball coach quote a poem that exemplified it very well,

No written word

Nor spoken plea

Can teach our youth

What they should be

Nor all the books

On all shelves

It's what the teachers

Are themselves[3]

As kids we most times copy the character of our parents. Same goes in leadership the followers most time emulate the character of the leader. People naturally do what they see if you are the leader that cheat, your followers cheats, if you steal they steals, if you cut corners they cut corners, if you are the type that comes late to the office the tendency of them coming late is there. Colin

ജ്ഞ

When you lead by example you become a sample too simple to locate

ജ്ഞ

Powell one time U.S secretary of states remarks "you can issue all the memos and give all the motivational speeches you want but if the rest of the people in your organization don't see you putting forth your very best effort every single day they won't either"

Great leaders like Gandhi understand these principles that is why he did not just lead his people but he led them by examples. He practiced what he teaches also became what he taught them; in Indian today his name has been immortalize. Your followers believe you more when you practice what you teach and teach what you practice.

VISIONARY LEADERS LIVE THE VISION

You don't become a visionary leader by having a vision. You don't become a visionary leader by believing your vision. You don't become a visionary leader by communicating your vision.

Don't get me wrong, having a vision, believing your vision, communicating your vision clearly, creatively, and continually are all good but them alone is not good enough to make it work. The leader also should live the vision. That is when you become the vision and the vision becomes you it is what makes the vision to come alive. Nelson Mandela lived the vision so was Gandhi same with Martin Luther King Jr.

That is while many years after his death U. S. still celebrate Martin Luther's day till date, it was what inspired the U.S. space program to fulfill John F. Kennedy's vision by putting a man in the moon. It is what makes followers to go to any length with their leader not minding the road blocks that surrounds it.

VISIONARY LEADERS BUILD GOOD RELATIONSHIP

Visionary leaders see people or their followers as their greatest assets. Friend it might interest you to note, good and mutual relationship are the spirit of effectual visionary leadership. A

Chinese proverb observed that:

If you want one year of prosperity grow grain, if you want ten year of prosperity grow trees, if you want one hundred years of prosperity grow people.

ഇൗൽ

Aaron Feuerstein CEO of Malden Mill understands this proverb very well that is while when fire destroyed 75% of his company he kept his entire employee on

Building a solid relationship in your organization helps your organization remain solid.

ഇൽ

the payroll. His employees were so happy that they helped him rebuild the company. Within a year, the company had more profit than ever.

Building a solid relationship in your organization helps your organization remain solid. In building a solid relationship with them you have create a core value and a strong partnership. Gone are the days when leadership command, pushes, bullies, and dominates followers no! Visionary leaders exhibit a great sense of respect for people that are following them and consciously and carefully develop a team spirit and team learning.

Building a solid relationship is important in building a solid leadership and having a solid leadership is important in having a solid relationship that is to say that the two are inseparable.

Looking at it this way, the leader is the compass and the followers are the body of the ship that carries the compass. The body can't work without the compass while the compass can't work without the ship both needs each other. This is how it is in leadership. Friend hear this, leadership is meaningless without followership and sustaining followership you need a solid, strong and vibrant relationship with your followers.

VISIONARY LEADERS LEAD BY MENTORING

Friend you never come across sports star without a coach, you never come across a professor of knowledge without once a student, and you never come across a leader of substance and worth without a mentor.

Every true Visionary leader leads by passing on the mantle of leadership by mentoring their followers. Friend hear this, you are the original copy of your mentor not a duplicated copy *"...the spirit of Elijah doth rest on me..."*

Your mentor gives you the mantle you desire to accomplish your divine assignment here on earth. Visionary leaders understand that mentorship is a fundamental law in leadership so they make themselves and every facility available to mentor their followers to fulfill destiny. Mentors are ladders in whose steps we engage to fulfill divine purpose.

We walk by common sense, run by principle, fly by instructions. Know matter how gifted the pilot is he must follow instructions to land safely, if he says NO! To instructions, well, you and I know what his fate will be.

Anybody who cannot instruct you is not your mentor, friend hear this, visionary leaders are not mentholated folds but mentors, some folds want mentholated leaders around them, something that makes them feel cool and ok, but not with true mentors.

ॐ

Mentors are ladders in whose steps we engage to fulfil divine purpose

ॐ

A mentor will not take you where you necessary want to be but ought to be. Most times their instructions might be outside your own box of idea why, because they have journeyed on that road before you.

I wrote my first book, very wonderful book by me and colleagues, I took it to my academic mentor Professor Charles deputy VC Covenant University Ota for endorsement while others are commenting on the book he took it after some weeks he called me I went to hear what he was going to say, I got to his office he waited patiently for me that day he said told me "wisdom you tried giving your time to write but your work is not good enough for me to endorse for these reasons I will not give you my endorsement" what! That was what went through my mind; I didn't bother to take it to other of my mentors because they will still see what he saw. He gave me his reasons and told me what to do and how to write I applied all that he taught me that day in his office in all my subsequent books, sincerely if I didn't adhere to what he taught me I would have ruin this precious gift of writing

God gave me and my destiny.

Your mentors are your coach, they are there to tell you when to rest and when to train, you might want to rest but your coach says no, this is not the time to rest but to train. Friend hear this, what you discover will make the world discover you. Discover your mentor they are all around you waiting for your discovering so that your world will start discovering your worth, it takes a visionary leader to lead you to your discovering.

SEVEN PILLARS OF VISIONARY LEADERSHIP

These are the pillars that hold visionary leaderships and a true leader mentors their followers through this seven pillars.

Vision	I know where I am going
Mapping	I know how to get there
Journeying	I am willing to start
Learning	I am open to change
Mentoring	I am open to others
Leading	I will set an example
Valuing	I will do what is right

CHAPTER TWO

ATTITUDE

Attitude is everything in leadership. It is what determines your level of impact, growth, relationship and your followership. Friend hear this, when you are lacking in favor check your attitude and without positive attitude you can't make a positive impact in leadership and every sector of life.

Your breakthrough in leadership is highly determined by how far you have breakthrough in your attitude as a leader and it is the attitude of a leader most times that determines the attitude people we have towards the organization, when any organization is having an attitude challenges watch it, most time the person leading the organization is having an attitudinal challenge.

Friend hear this, it the aptitude of your attitude towards others that determines your altitude in leadership. The value system of leadership is meaningless if not the value a leader place on his attitude. Let's me put it clear- don't underestimate the power of a positive attitude.

Thomas Jefferson asserted "Nothing can stop the man with the right mental attitude from achieving his goal; nothing on earth can help the man with the wrong mental attitude ..."

Attitude is very important in leadership; it can make or unmake you. Stories of great leaders both death and alive came as a result of right mental attitude towards themselves and the people around them, it is your attitude that will determine the kind of success you will attract as an individual, team, organization etc.

You will agree with me that everything operates by law of cause and effect. Success is assured when we live on the right mental attitude.

Negative attitude = Negative result

Positive attitude = Positive result

Good attitude = Good result

Fair attitude = Fair result

Poor attitude = Poor result

Think about these things. Friends, success in leadership or in any organization is caused more by mental attitude then mental capacity.

PARETO PRINCIPLES

An Italian economist by name Vilfredo Pareto created a mathematical formula describing the unequal distribution of wealth. He observed that twenty percent of people controlled or owned eighty percent of the wealth in the late 9040s, a quality business management consultant Dr. Joseph M. Juran attributed the 80-20 rule also known as the law of the vital few and the principle of factor sparsity to Pareto calling "*Pareto*" principle"[1]

This states that for any events roughly 80% of the effects come from 20% of the causes. Looking at the diagram below will give us

a clear picture of what it means

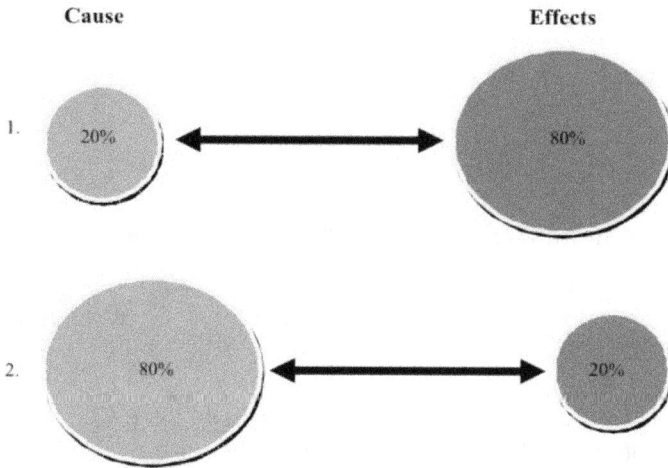

Cause   Effects

Looking at the diagram above the first represents a leader, or organization who spends their most precious Time, Energy, Money to build the most important aspect of their attitude in relationship to their organizational growth the result is four or more fold return in productivity while the second represents a CEO that spend the same time, energy, and money on the most insignificant or place less priorities on the most important aspect of his attitude the result will be small in the organizational growth.

ଛଏଔ

It is the aptitude of your attitude towards others that determines your altitude in leadership.

ଛଏ ଔ

The leadership of any organization has a responsibility to determine the few people 20 percent in their organization that have the right attitude that will deliver result but before that, the leader must have worked on himself before he can work on his followers.

LITERAL EXAMPLES OF PARETO PRINCIPLE

20 % of your character determines 80% of your attitude

20% of your attitude produces 80% of your altitude

20% of people around you determine 80% of the company you keep

20% of people will make 80% of the decision

20% of your ideas produce 80% of your results

20% of your work determines 80% of your satisfaction

20% of your environment will make 80% of your life

20% of the books you read will determine 80% of your behavior.

Every leader should understand Pareto in the area of followership. For example, there's a reason that only 20% of people do well and 80% do not the reason is not Talent, Gifts, Potential, Money, or being at the right place at the right time, the only reason is attitude.

Friend, only with positive mental attitude can one achieves results.

HOW A LEADER LOCATES THE 20% IN AN ORGANIZATION

Identifying the twenty percent that have the right mental positive attitude about life in the organization is very simple if the leader follows these steps:

If the person should leave the organization will his absence be felt?
Yes ☐   No ☐

If the person should take a negative action against the organization will it be seen?
Yes ☐   No ☐

Does the person presence build the organization positively or negativdy?
Yes ☐   N o ☐

Does the person have a team spirit to work with his colleagues around?
Yes ☐   No ☐

Does the person idea meant to build or meant to criticize the work force?
Yes ☐   No ☐

Does the person takes advice even when it is not conducive to him but for the good of the organization?
Yes ☐   No ☐

Can the person take correction without feeling naughty?
Yes ☐   No ☐

Can the person work outside his or her own box?
Yes ☐   No ☐

Role the person plays in your organization does him or she has a capable replacement?
Yes ☐   No ☐

Does the person work to earn wages or make impart in and through the organization?
Yes ☐   No ☐

These and more are some of the ways you can identify the 20% of the work force in your organization. Friend hear this; if their presence does not make any impart their absence will not make any difference.

We have been in a team where one of the team members among us always look at the glass with half empty and others will look at it with half full the one that looks at half empty is always first to complain while it will not work but at the end it does work. The truth still remains if they can't make it or cope with your ideas it is better you bid them farewell for the growth of the organization.

Ability to say No! Farewell! Goodbye! Is what make one a leader sometimes. Tony Blair said "The art of leadership is saying no, not yes. It is very easy to say yes." I have observed in life any issue you are facing at the moment is not as significant as your attitude toward it, because it's what determines your success or failure in life. The way you respond to the issue will either defeat you before you ever do anything about it. You can be defeated by that issue because you think you are. So think!

Anything you think about your attitude is obviously true about yourself because you are going to produce after your thoughts. Mary Kay Ash summed it up this way "if you think you can, you can. And if you think you can't, you are right."

You may have heard this story before, many years ago before Africa became what it is today two British salesmen a shoe manufacturing company sent them to Africa to investigate and report back on market potential.

The first salesman reported back, *"there is a massive potential here nobody wears shoes."*

The second salesman reported back *"there is no potential here nobody wears shoes."*

Both of them went for the same thing but they saw differently the second saw negative the first saw positive that is opportunity why, it is only their mental attitude that makes the difference. Friend, positive attitude is what makes you see the vision, believe the vision, and delivers the vision. Take your time and ponder over this poem it explained it very well.

I am obedient servant

Whatever you ask me to

Do I will do it with all

My heart.

Ask me to sleep,

That is what I enjoy doing

Ask me to work

That is my way of life

Ask me to gossip

Lol! You have touch the

Best part of me.

Ask me to play,

Wow! That is where I

Win awards

Ask me to lead,

Wonderful! Leadership

Is my life.

Ask me to follow

I'm called a steward

Who are I?

Hahaha! Am attitude

I will do anything you

Ask me to do…

Friend, attitude is everything in leadership and life. You can't gain much from life when you have a negative attitude towards life and you can't gain anything from your organization when you see things from the negative side of life.

ഇ)രു

Whatever you set your mind to see that you are prepared to see, I love what William James says "the greatest revolution of our generation is the discovery that human beings, by changing the inner attitude of their minds, can change the outer aspects of their lives."

Attitude is what help you see challenges as the necessary things to come to give you the necessary things you need. It is what makes you see challenge as your next door to your breakthrough.

CHANGE IT

A story was told, an old blind man was sitting on a busy street corner in the rush-hour begging for money on a cardboard sign, next to an empty tin cup, he had written "blind please help." No one was giving him any money.

A young advertising writer walked past and saw the blind man with his sign and empty cup, and also saw many people passing by completely unmoved, let alone stopping to give money. The advertising writer took a thick marking pen from her pocket, turned the cardboard sheet back to front and rewrote the sign, then went on her way.

After awhile, when the cup was overflowing the blind man asked a stranger to tell him what the sign now said. The stranger replied *"it says it's a beautiful day; you can see it I cannot."* Friend, am here to tell you is a beautiful day you may not see it but I can see it.

You can rewrite the negative attitude of yours, yes! You can!! Is as simple as you least expected all you need to do is change the books you read, the friends you keep, it might interest you to note that twenty children cannot play together for twenty years. As you know, change is the only thing that is constant, change what you listen to, change what you watch, the CD's, DVD's etc. change where you always go to, if it is not benefiting your attitude positively, change! Change!! Change!!! Friend you can change it, you can change your attitude, you can rewrite your destiny, you can realize your dreams, visions, goals, you have a mission on earth here don't allow challenges to knock you down. Friend hear this; attitude is what help you see challenges as the necessary things to come to give you the necessary things you need. It is what makes you see challenge as your next door to your breakthrough.

Chuck Swindoll says "the longer we live, the more I realize the impart of attitude on life. Attitude to me is more important than facts. It is more important than past, than education, than money, than circumstances, than failures, than success, than what other people think or say or do. It is more important than appearance, Gift, or Skill. It will make or break a company....a church...a home. The remarkable thing is we have choice everyday regarding the attitude we will embrace for that day. We cannot change our past... we cannot change the fact that people will act in a certain way. We cannot change the inevitable. The only thing we can do is to play on the string we have, and that is our attitude. I am convinced that life is 10 percent what happens to me and 90 percent how I react to it. And so it is with you...we are in charge of our attitude" you can change your attitude but is up to you.

BECOME LIKE THIS FROG

This is fairy-tale; there was a bunch of tiny frogs who arranged a running competition the goal was to reach the top of a very high tower. A crowd gathered around the tower to see the race and cheer on the contestants...the race began...honestly nobody in the crowd believes that any frog would reach the top of the tower. There were statements like "oh, the way too difficult!! They will never reach to top of the tower oh! Can't you see the tower is too high the tiny frog began to collapse one by one.... except for those who in a fresh tempo were climbing higher and higher. The crowd continued to yell it is too difficult! No one will make it, tinier frog got tired and gave up...but one more continued higher and higher and higher.... This one wouldn't give up! At the end everyone else had given up climbing the tower. Except for the one tiny frog that after a big effort was the only one who reached the top. When all of the other tiny frogs wanted to know how this one frog managed to do it, a contestant asked the tiny frog "how he who has succeeded has found the straight to reach the top?" it turnout that the winner was deaf...

Friend, never allow the negative statements or opinion of people around you sometime to determine your results in life in that way they will take the most in important virtue that matter from you and that is your positive mental attitude toward life. Hear this people can take your money, mansion, conglomerate, cars, etc but don't allow them to take the most important thing in your life that is, your attitude because with it you can gain all that was lost double.

You need to become deaf as that tiny frog if your organization must climb the ladder of success. Getting to the tower of your organization does not requires money, energy etc all of them are good but the most important thing is attitude.

Attitude is what says you can when everything around you says you can't. Be deaf when people say you can't either by suggestion, questions, advice, examples etc. you can only if you allow your attitude. Whatever attitude you give to life the same will life give to you even more. Let's try to look at attitude in its acronym

A – Attraction
 T –Teamwork
  T –Team spirit
   I –Influence
    T –Teachable
     U –Unbelievable results
      D –Dependable
       E –Example

ATTRACTION

Can your attitude attract people to you? Definitely it will, but the issues are will it attract positive minded individuals? Friend hear this, what you attract determines what you are what you are determines what you attract and receives. You will agree with me that like beget like. The attitude you possess will determine what you will possess from life.

TEAMWORK

Does your attitude build teamwork or does it repel followership from you and the organization? When a team works together they win together, succeed together and get to the top together. Andrew Carnegie said "team work is the ability to work together towards a common vision and the ability to direct individual accomplishments towards organization objectives. It is the fuel that allows common people to attain uncommon results". Henry Ford observed "Coming together is a beginning. Keeping together is progress. Working together is success" You know numerically one plus one is two but in teamwork 1+1=11. That is the power of teamwork.

TEAM SPIRIT

Does your attitude build a team spirit or does it build negativity, Strife, Envy, Gossip Malice etc among the work force? "Can two works together except they agree...?" (Amos 3:3) before you work as a team your spirit must have concluded about it. John C. Maxwell says "A team doesn't win the championship if its players are working from different agendas."[2]

looking at this statement the other way; a team does not win a championship if they are operating with different spirit. Buchholz and Roth asserted "wearing the same shirts doesn't make a team" Any organization your spirit does not accept, your best can't show there.

INFLUENCE

Does your attitude influence people around you positively or negatively? As we all know that influence is leadership. When your attitude cannot influence people check your character. Your character has much to say about your leadership style and your result of your organization.

When you are lacking in character your influence towards your followers positively will be very low. Though, you might be influencing them the other way round.

TEACHABLE

Do you have a teachable spirit; can people around you learn something good from your attitude? What you learn makes you and your attitude is the sum total of your identity. People around see your identity through your behavioral

ഇ**C**ൽ

A teachable heart is a growing mind and a growing mind is a superstar in the making.

ഇ**C**ൽ

attitude, friend a teachable heart is a growing mind and a growing mind is a superstar in the making.

UNBELIEVABLE RESULTS

Does your attitude show a tenacious, unrelenting behavior towards challenges of life or does it show a wavering attitude towards issues of life? Does your attitude always eager to feel the invisible, touch the intangible, and achieve the impossible? Friend, attitude is what make you see impossible as I'm-possible. In recent times one of the living icons in soccer, a coach whose name sounds more then the players when he was the coach of Real Madrid Jose Mourinho (the special one) as he is fondly called, in his media speech made this statements "I am prepared the more pressure there is the stronger I am. In Portugal, we say the bigger the ship, the stronger the storm. Fortunately for me, I have always been in big ships. FC Porto was a very big ship in Portugal, Chelsea was also a big ship in England and Inter was a great ship in Italy. Now I'm at real Madrid, which is considered the biggest ship on the planet he also said "…. *fear is not a word in my football dictionary.*" you can get unbelievable result by conquering fear that is how great leaders get their results.

DEPENDABLE

Can people around depend on your attitude; can your followers trust your character? If they can't depend on you they can't depend on your leadership. J. R. Miller once observed "the only thing that walks back from the tomb with the mourners and refuses to be buried is the character of the man." This is true. What a man is survives him. It can never be buried.

EXAMPLE

Can what you teach represent what you live or if the two should come close will they recognize themselves. When what you teach does not represent what you live you are only leader by mouth. Friend, it is your character that will determine how solid your leadership will be. Your followers catch your character fester than your words and leadership is better behaved then teaches. If your attitude cannot set the example your altitude will be very low, Friend, your aptitude is what defines your character, your character is your attitude, and your attitude is what determines your altitude. Example is the key for effective leadership. Lead by example and become a better sample for others.

WE ARE RESPONSIBLE FOR OUR ATTITUDE

An advisor to President Lincoln suggested a certain candidate for the like Lincoln cabinet but Lincoln refused, saying "I don't the man's face"

But, sir, "he can't be responsible for his face," insisted the advisor. Lincoln replied "every man over forty is responsible for his face." That was the end of that matter. Our attitude toward any issues will always show on our face. Friend, change your attitude your world will change. The day you decide to take control of your life is the greatest day of your life.

I came across this story during my research "there once was a woman who woke up one morning, looked in the mirror and noticed she had only three hairs on her head.

"Well," she said "I think I'll braid my hair today. So she did and she had a wonderful day. The next day she woke up, looked in the mirror and saw that she had only two hairs on her head. "H-m-m," she said, "I think I'll part my hair down the middle today?"

So she did and she had grand day. The next day she woke up, looked in the mirror and noticed that she had only one hair on her head. "Well," she said, "today I'm going to wear my hair in a pony tail.

So she did and she had a fun, fun day. The next day she woke up looked in the mirror and noticed that there wasn't a single hair on her head.

"YEA" she exclaimed, "I don't have to fix my hair today."[3]

You are hundred percent in charge of your attitude, how you want to see it is what you will see. Friends, take charge of your attitude positively and start changing your world positively it all depends on you and the ability within you that is your will power. Einstein observed, "There is a driving force more powerful then steam, electricity and atomic energy...the will."

ജാ

Friends, your aptitude is what defines your character, your character is your attitude, and your attitude is what determines your altitude.

ജാ

CHAPTER THREE

LOYALTY

L oyalty in leadership cannot be compromise in any organization that desires growth. It is a very important virtue in leadership and it's among the things that have the ability to take you from down to up both in human life and the organization. Loyalty is not what a leader pretends to leave with. Pretence will only give a part time result not a permanent result.

I have discovered that Loyalty its origin is human heart the centre of self respect, honour and human decorum which cannot be design by human making either manufactured or produced on an assembly line. It is a force which has no capacity to jump into

ഇ)C

Loyalty is that love portion any follower that desires growth and motion can give his boss.

ഇ)C

person until the conditions are exactly right for it and it is a force capable of detecting infidelity. Friend, that is why loyalty is the key for any great height you desire in life.

FROM A CLASS TEACHER TO COMMANDER-IN-CHIEF

A young class teacher joined politics officially in 1998 to a particular party, because of his transparent loyalty in 1999 he became a deputy governor of his state, and he was so loyal to his boss that it was so obvious to everybody in the state including the opposition party and the generality of the country. His boss loved him. Loyalty is that love portion any follower that desires growth and motion can give his boss.

After their first tenure in office his boss took him again to contest for the sit the second time fortunately for them they won the election he was still very loyal to his boss during that period his boss had challenges with the powers that be which lead to his removal from office as the executive governor of that state the mantle of leadership was then saddled on this young man he refused to take over power until it was cleared that he is the only person that is qualified to be on that sit base on the constitution of the country he took over as the executive governor of that state but was still very loyal to his boss and still called him *"my boss."*

At the expiration of that tenure he wanted to officially contest for office of the executive governor but the powers that be have taken note of his unrelenting loyalty to his boss and called him to be a running mate of the presidential candidate of their party this is something he has not planned even if he has a plan for it is not now he vehemently refused the offer and said *"I am not interested please"* the party unanimously said *"you are the only person that will pair the presidential candidate"* after much pressure he obediently accept the offer fortunately for them they won the presidential race he became the vice president before the end of that tenure his new boss became ill and he was flown abroad for medical treatment which lasted for months but this humble steward was not eager to take over power and was still very loyal to his new boss even when he offer to see his boss he was refused entry.

A motion from the senate on the 9th of February 2010 confirmed him to act as the president the same month his boss came back he was very willing to hand over power to his boss but the health condition of his boss could not allow him to take over power few months later, on the 5th of may
2010 his boss passed on.

ഇ)ര

On the 6th of May he took oath of office as the president after nine months in office an official election was conducted which was believed to be free and fair by

Loyalty is what determines your royalty in life.

ഇ)ര

local and international communities which he gallantly won and became the first person to head such position in his region a man who did not come from the families of who is who in his country and a son of ordinary farmer, his is the former President, Commander-in-Chief of Arm Forces of Federal Republic of Nigeria. Dr Goodluck Ebele Azikiwe Jonathan (*GCFR*).

Friends hear this, there is nothing loyalty can't give you and there is nothing disloyalty can't take from you. Loyalty is a key that has ability to unlock you to unimaginable experiences, loyalty is what determines your royalty in life, it has the ability to take you from **here** to **there** the only difference of these two words is "**T**" which stands for time.

Are you under somebody? Am telling you just be loyal to your boss in any environment you find yourself be it organization, church, mosque etc give yourself time you will get there. Looking at this diagram below explained it very well.

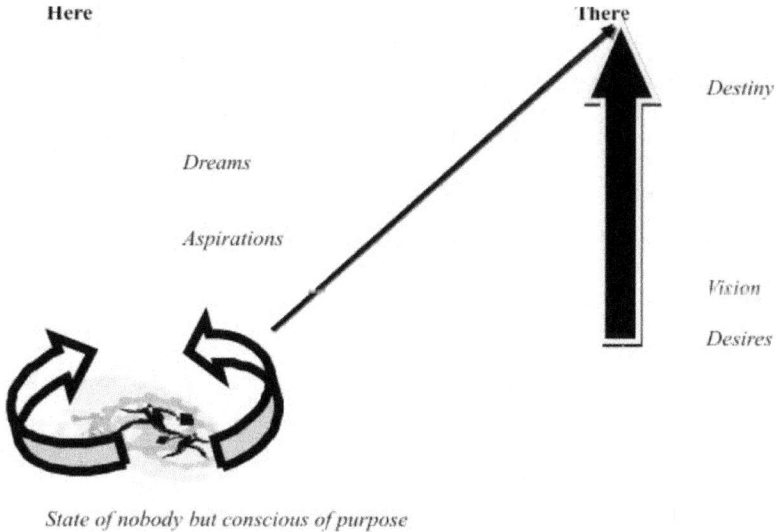

Here   **There**

Destiny

Dreams

Aspirations

Vision

Desires

State of nobody but conscious of purpose

Getting to the top requires patience, determination, and coupled with enthusiasm you will definitely get to the top, Elbert Hubbard observed "An ounce of loyalty is worth a pound of cleverness." No matter how smart you are or you want to play, friend, without loyalty your success is limited in leadership and issues of life. Skills, Smartness, Authority etc are all good but if you must scale new height in leadership or any organization you need an ounce of loyalty.

TWO WAY THING

Loyalty is not a one way traffic is a value character trait between the leader and the follower, between the employer and the employee. Grace Murray Hopper asserted "Leadership is a two-way street, loyalty up and loyalty down. Respect for one's superiors; care for one's crew."

Friend hear this; loyalty is the glue that holds relationship solidly together. Any CEO that desires loyalty from his or her subordinate must be ready to be loyal to them as well. Among other things relationship in organization, team, or friendship is sustained or broken because of loyalty. Without loyalty leadership will not stand the test of time, it is the oil that keeps relationship, organization, or a team going. It is something like this....

Leadership   **Followership**

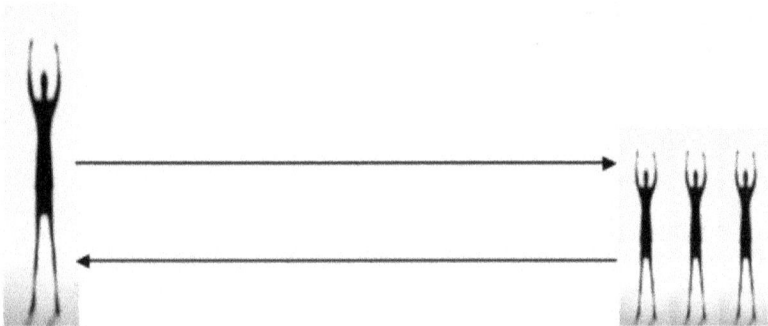

You give they reciprocate.

Donald T. Regan remarks "you've got to give loyalty down, if you want loyalty up" loyalty is a give and take magic. If you the CEO are loyal the tendency of the 80% of your work force will be loyal to you. Chapter two of this book gives explanation of these 80/20 Pareto principle very well. Loyalty is allegiance to a group of person or cause. It means coming down to their level relating in their own language. Lee J. Iacocca observed "talking to people in their own language. If you do it well, they'll say, "God, he said exactly what I was thinking? And when they begin to respect you, they'll follow you to the death." Any solid relationship is built on a solid loyalty most especially from the leadership.

Loyalty is the bedrock of any healthy relationship and both leadership and loyalty should go in the same parallel line and any leader that fail to understand this simple formula will not stand the test of time no doubt. And understand when it comes to loyalty the rule is you will not give what you can't receive.

Enjoying progress in life and any sector of life is very simple if you can appreciate this principle you should understand that you are a "leader" not a "dictator" and what are the traits of a true leader is influence and how do you influence them? Is only by these character traits, integrity, positive attitude, humility, loyalty etc.

Leadership does not make you a genius it only makes you a servant to help service the need of your followers

In my continent Africa there is a leadership challenge because the so called leaders in quotes don't understand this character traits of a leader or they do but they don't want to live with it they expect their country to be loyal to them but they are not willing and ready to be loyal to the constitution of their country they have even gone ahead to change the constitution in fact, they have become the constitution themselves, take for example what happened in Libya. Leadership does not make you a genius it only makes you a servant to help service the need of your followers. Friend, you can only influence positively when you have been positively influenced inwardly which expresses itself outwardly. Some African leaders do not understand that being in leadership position is not a do or die affair but a do and serve affair.

President of Libya was killing his own people just to remain in power because he failed to understand the whole essence of leadership. Friend, are you a leader or dictator? You can know this by how they respect you or how they fear you. If in your organization, they fear you instead of respect you watch it you might be a dictator not a leader. Algernon Charles observed "whenever there is a grain of loyalty there is a glimpse of freedom" you see a true freedom where there is a true leader. Hans Seliye says "leaders are leaders only as long as they have the respect and loyalty of their followers."[1]

Whatever you desire from your followers be the first to give it out. You set the example others follow this is what leadership demands.

QUALITIES OF LOYALTY

Any of these qualities is very important in leadership they are the bedrock in leadership and loyalty is the glue that holds all of them together. When your leadership styles miss these

ഹോൽ

Leadership positions is not a do or die affair but a do and serve affair.

ഓഗ

qualities you might have quantity but certainly not quality. You

44

don't enjoy quality leadership until you lay hold on some of these quality rudiments of leadership.

TRUST

Everybody, organizations speak trust but friend, trust is not just a word we say but is a word we should live on and practice and you don't command trust you earn the trust of your followers. Warren Bennis and Burt Nanus in their book *"leaders' strategies for taking charges"* called trust the glue that binds followers and leaders together" I believe is not wise to tell your followers you must trust me, that is wrong. They can only trust you when your character says so not your mouth. Friend, nothing builds confidence in organization like trust when your followers trust you they work with you confidently. The good thing about trust in any organization is, when you trust them *(followers)* you open their creativity when they trust you they give their best.

HOW TO BUILD TRUST

- ➤ Practice what you say and do.
- ➤ Don't betray your followers.
- ➤ Say the truth always even when it is not favorable to you.
- ➤ Believe them when they tell you something most time.
- ➤ Don't gossip or criticize them in their absence.
- ➤ Criticize their work constructively if you must do.
- ➤ Believe in their ideas, potentials, gifts, talents.
- ➤ Become a friend to them indeed and in need. When they relate their personal issues to you do take them serious.

In that way you have created a channel of absolute loyalty in your work force. Without

Trust your follower's loyalty is only in paper not character.

HONESTY

Thomas Jefferson once said "honesty is the first chapter of the book of wisdom" how honest are you both to yourself and your followers? No leader builds a solid organization by dishonesty means and hear this, dishonesty will create big disloyalty and honesty will build great loyalty among your followers. A dishonest leader is not destined to greatness in any form.

True honesty is that which reflect in everything about you. Looking at this description below:

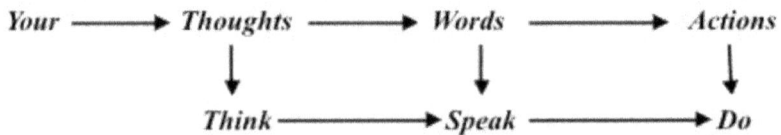

Your ⟶ *Thoughts* ⟶ *Words* ⟶ *Actions*

Think ⟶ *Speak* ⟶ *Do*

It is to speak that which is thought and do that which is spoken where there is no contradiction or discrepancies in thoughts, words, or action. Loyalty is possible when your honesty can be seen through your thoughts, words, or actions. Honesty is to say the truth the way it is without adding to it or removing from it.

Mark Twain observed "if you tell the truth you don't have to remember anything" truth is truth take it anywhere you like. Many CEO are having challenges in their organization because they are not honest to their employees and you don't expect result when you keep living a dishonest life either by cheating or lying. Abraham Lincoln asserted "No man has a good enough memory to make a successful liar" lies gives you a temporally solution not a permanent solution. Lying is like building on sinking sand Proverb 20:23, 17 observed *"what you get by dishonesty you may enjoy like finest food, but sooner or later it will be like a mouth full of sands."*

Friend, honesty is one of the keys that opens door of loyalty among

ಱಂಡಃ

When you pay attention to your integrity your followers will pay attention to your commands and instructions.

ಱಂಡಃ

your equals and your followers, live to be honest, people will live to be loyal to you.

INTEGRITY

This is when what you think, say, and do are the same, when your public and private life should meet themselves and recognizes each other. No CEO enjoys the loyalty of their followers when they lack integrity. It is integrity that makes a leader earn the trust and loyalty of their followers. Whatever the leadership show is what the followers will reflect.

Value system of leadership is about placing value of the most important area of our leadership when you don't place value on your integrity you might want to do anything and believing you will get away with it. Friend hear this, when you pay attention to your integrity your followers will pay attention to your commands and instructions.

At a time in my life I have this integrity challenge when what I do and what I say do not reflect my identity, I realized that my words do not carry weight as it ought I started checking myself I noticed where the challenge lies I worked at myself, I made up my mind that what I feel, thinks, says, and do, must align with each other. At this point, my life started regaining it self-esteem and worth. Friend, leading without integrity is leading in shame. You can enjoy the support of your followers when they see that.

Leading without integrity is leading in shame.

What you think ➡ *what you say* ➡ *and what you do*

Align with each other that is, when you are a leader by character not charisma. Leadership by charisma is leading without foundation but integrity is the foundation of every true leadership. Understanding the value system of leadership your foundation must be solid and that is your integrity. Pat Williams tells a story in his book *"American Scandal"* about Mahatma Gandhi's trip to England to speak before the parliament. British Government have vehemently refused Indian independence, Gandhi being the front line advocate for independence has many times be jailed, arrested, and threatened as a result. Spoke passionately and eloquently for almost two hours without any note. After which the parliament gave him a standing ovation. Later, a reporter asked Gandhi's assistance, Mahadav Desai how this elder statesman was able to deliver such a powerful speech without a note.

"You don't understand Gandhi" Desai responded. "You see, what he thinks is what he feels. What he feels is what he says. What he says is what he does. What Gandhi feels, what he thinks, what he says, and what he does are all the same. He does not need notes"

Margaret Mead cultural anthropologist stated "what people say, what people do, and what people say they do are entirely different things" this is very obvious for leaders who lead without character and integrity.

Friend, this is when there is no compromise in leadership when everything is in a parallel line with each other. Friend, becoming a leader without developing a good character is making a shipwreck of leadership, it is integrity in leadership that makes one commands the loyalty of your followers or people around you.

Pride is a great and a big humiliation on your road to destiny.

PRIDE A VITAL ENEMY OF LOYALTY

I am yet to see any proud leader that is loyal lol! Is like mixing oil with water the two can't work or mix together is either you are proud or you are loyal. Pride is a powerful force that keeps one from being loyal to people around him or her. It is that inner witness that tells you that you are better than everybody around you there is nothing you can gain from their ideas you better go ahead with your plans. Dave Anderson, speaker and author believes that number one cause of failure in management is pride he writes

"There are many reason managers fail. For some, the organization outgrows them. Others don't change with times…A few make poor character choices. They look good for a while but eventually discover they can't get out of their own way. Increasingly more keep the wrong people too long because they don't want to admit they made a mistake or have high turnover become a negative reflection on them. Some failures had brilliant past track records but start using their success as a license to build a fence around what they had rather than continue to risk and stretch to build it to even higher levels. But all these causes for management failure have their root in one common cause: Pride

In simplest terms, pride is devastating…. the pride that inflates your sense of self-worth and distorts your perspective of reality."

Pride makes a leader looks like a very big balloon beautifully designed but inside is only air a small tiny pin can puncture it.

Pride gives you a wrong picture of yourself worth accompanied by a distorted perspective of the reality. Muammar Gaddafi could not see the present reality that his people are tired of his government even when they started rioting he felt that he has what it takes to stop them but all in his military acumen failed him he ran out of the capital Tripoli and went into hiding, finally on the 20th of October 2011 he was killed. Pride closes your eyes to the reality of life. Friend, pride is a great and a big humiliation on your road to destiny. Pride can take you there but loyalty keeps you there. And hear this, if you don't deal with pride it will deal with you with time.

Proverb observed "Do you see a man who is wise in his own eyes? There is more hope for a fool than for him" (Proverb. 26:12). Pride prevents you from seeing new ideas and the present reality. Friend you can say no! To pride and embrace humility it does not take much to subdue it as Benjamin Franklin

ఎంౘ

Pride gives you a wrong picture of yourself worth accompanied by a distorted perspective of the reality.

ఎంౘ

observed, "There is perhaps not one of our natural passions so hard to subdue as pride. Beat it down, stifle it, mortify it as much as one pleases, it is still alive. Even if I could conceive that I had completely overcome it, I should probably be proud of my humility."

HOW DO I OVERCOME IT?

You first of all accept you have it, and start looking for the areas of your life is very predominant because some that have it don't know themselves most times. Friend, the antidote to pride is to embrace humility. C. S. Lewis remarked, "If anyone would like to

51

acquire humility, I can, I think, tell him the first step. The first step is to realize that one is proud. And a biggish step, too. At least, nothing whatever can be done before it. If you think you are not conceited, you are very conceited indeed."

Saxon white Kissinger poem has change my perspective about my entire life as an individual it is called *"Indispensable man"* anytime I feel am very important, better than everybody around, without me it can't be done, the most qualified candidate, etc. I go back to my sheave and read it. It says:

Sometime when you're feeling important;

Sometime when your ego's in bloom

Sometime when you take it for granted

You're the best qualified in the room

Sometimes when you feel that your going

Would leave an unfillable hole,

Just follow these simple instructions

And see how they humble your soul;

Take a bucket and fill it with water

Put your hand in it up to the wrist,

Pull it out and the hole that's remaining

Is a measure of how you'll be missed.

You can splash all you wish when you either,

You may stir up the water galore

But stop and you'll find that in no time

It looks quite the same as before.

The moral of this quaint example

Is do just the best that you can,

Be proud of yourself but remember,

There's no indispensable man

This poem anytime I come across it, it makes me loyal always and makes me realize am not indispensable man.

On that fateful Sunday 26 October 2003 we all gathered in our local church to worship God we were told the sad news that our resident pastor has gone to be with the Lord I could not believe it I thought it was a dream but is obviously real I wept all through. This is a man that has mentored many brethren, loved by many and have planted many churches both home and abroad the last he did was South African church. The day of his burial people came from all works of life I was privileged to be among the ushers that served that day, what surprises me was, this my late beloved pastor was still lying in state people that was shedding tears have started asking for rice, chicken, etc friends, the world will not stop if anything should happen to you now. Some folds believed, that was the end of that ministry but is still waxing very strong, even stronger.

Friend, in funerals you hear words like this "the deceased have left vacuum nobody else can feel, He left indelible mark here on earth" etc such statements are not always true, and that should not make you think oh! Am important and become proud of yourself. Friend, loyalty is the key to greatness.

ℰℭ

Loyalty is the key to greatness.

Life has taught me to embrace loyalty no matter the environment I found myself

ℰℭ

because it is the ladder to great heights in life. I have always make it a point in my life to be loyal to my superiors not minding the circumstances that surrounds me even people I feel I am better off now. Friends', being a leader is good but being a leader in loyalty is best. Remember what Kessinger said "**No indispensable man.**"

CHAPTER FOUR

UNIQUE LEADERSHIP

U nique leadership demands a lot from you as a leader which include your time, resources, energy, emotions etc. friend, you don't become a unique leader when you have not uniquely worked on yourself as an individual in your:

> ➢ Character
> ➢ Believe system
> ➢ Speech
> ➢ Approach to issues of life
> ➢ And the environment you stay

All these say a lot about your uniqueness as a leader. God creates every individual in a unique manner that only you have what it takes to bring it into reality. Every leader carries something in him or her that makes him unique but is the responsibility of the leader to locate it and the responsibility of the followers to align themselves with what the leader has located.

You will agree with me that lineol Messi of F.C. Barcelona was born to play soccer well, not many will disagree with this, am not saying he wouldn't have succeeded in any other thing if he didn't discover his unique ability no! But he would not have attained to this level of success and stardom he is enjoying today.

What is unique ability?

➢ It is the ability, skill, and talent that we were born with.

➢ It is the natural mineral resources that came with us at birth

➢ It is that our potential that makes us different from others around us.

Messi, had to cultivate, develop, practice and improve his "unique ability" on a daily bases to become great, but the ability was already within him and the interesting thing about this is he discovered it at every young age. I said "what you discover will make the world discover you". You might

Until you discover who you are men will not discover what you carry

have wonderful potentials within you but if you don't discover it and tap from it you remain a wonderer. We carry a special unique skill in us but if you don't work at it you remain where you are. Tap your unique ability you enjoy affluence as a result of influence. Friend, what is your unique ability? You must discover what it is if you must influence effectively well. It might interest you to note until you lay hold on your unique potential nothing worthwhile lay holds on your destiny.

Become unique in your field, train and retrain yourself is very important if you must remain important.

"Feliz Navidad" we sing every Christmas was written by a blind man at a time blind people do nothing than stay at the corner of the road and beg for money he said no and start taping into his unique ability inline to divine purpose, he found an old guitar and started practicing on how to play it, day and night until he improved and his fingers bled. He taught himself how to play guitar today he is one of the greatest musician of our time his name is "Jose Feliciano". Friend, until you discover who you are men will not discover what you carry. Unique leadership is discovering that area of your skill, talent and gifting inline to divine purpose that is what makes you an influential leader. That is becoming unique in all facet of your life as an individual.

> *Until you lay hold on your unique potential nothing worthwhile lay holds on your destiny*

Unique leadership

- ➢ The character traits that makes you powerful or influential as a leader
- ➢ It is that special thing in you that makes you special
- ➢ It is what sets you apart from your equals
- ➢ It is that area of your strength you have developed inline to your leadership
- ➢ This is a leader that has developed positive values that keeps him strong and makes him enjoy influence
- ➢ This is a leader who have a peculiar trait he keeps in touch on a daily basis.

Friend, understand that what makes us unique is more than talents, gifts it is vigorously tied into our potentials. Discovery your potential in leadership is what makes you potent always.

Every leader carries with it a potential, and know that your potential does not come around you it comes from within you. Edward young remarks "we are all born originals, why is it so many of us die copies."[1]

Value system makes you understand that you have a unique ability, unique leadership styles, unique way of doing things with this understanding you have a unique responsibility to make your followers discover their unique ability by giving them responsibility inline to their unique strengths with this you are developing unique leaders that will take over from you.

Discovery your potential in leadership is what makes you potent always.

Friend, what make you unique leader is in your ability to go extra-mill to ordinary men that followed you in that way they become extraordinary men and women. David took with him vain men, ordinary men but at the end they became giants in their individual fields that is leadership.

Traits of unique leadership

Every great leader possesses some great traits that makes them great and remain great. We will explore some few traits of unique leaders they are:

Self belief

Winston Churchill: self confidence if you ask me was another name of this great man. His belief was a key in his leadership trait. This man belief not only in his abilities but his destiny. During his early days at school he would confidently tell his school mates that one day he would come to London's aid when the capital was under attack. Later, on his way in to battle for the first time in 1887 he wrote his mother "I have faith in my stay- that I am intended to do something in this world"[2]

Winston Churchill was told by gunnery expert captain Percy Scott, "I feel certain that I shall some day shake hands with you as prime minister of England; you possess the two necessary qualifications genius and plod combined I believe nothing can keep them back" whatever this statement did to Churchill I wouldn't know but I know it wouldn't have dimmed his self belief.

> *Men that have confidence in their dream can die but they don't go to the grave with their dreams, it will always out leave them.*

Abraham Lincoln: was raised in a very small family background had many failures in life; he lost three of his sons at a tender age. Robert Todd, the eldest, was the only one of the children to survive to adulthood, and lost in politics many times but all these did not make him to lose sight of his self confidence. He believed there is something he came to do on this world and that is to abolish slavery in the world with that he personally taught himself, and began reading Blackstone's Commentaries on the law of

England and other books and became a lawyer. He stated "I studied with nobody", he his known to be one of the best president united states have ever had.

His self belief that one day the blacks will be free started seeing the light of the day on June 19, 1862, congress passed an act banning slavery on all federal territory, and July 1862 passed the second confiscation act, which set up a court procedure that could free the slaves of anyone convicted of aiding the rebellion. Although Lincoln believed it was not within the power of the congress to free the slave within the state, he approved the bill in deference to the legislature. He felt such action can only be taken by the commander in-chief using power war granted to president by the constitution, and Lincoln was planning to take that action. In that month, Lincoln discussed a draft of the emancipation proclamation with his cabinet. In it, he stated that "as a fit and necessary military measure, on January 1, 1863, all person held as slave in the confederate states will thenceforward, and forever, be free."[3]

Privately, Lincoln concluded at this point that war could not be won without freeing the slaves. However, confederate and anti-war propagandist had success spreading the theme that emancipation was a stumbling block to peace and reunification. Republican editor Horace Greeley of highly influential *New York Tribune* fell the ploy.[4]

And Lincoln refuted it directed in a shrewd letter of August 22, 1862. The president said the primary goal of his actions as president (he used the first person pronoun and explicitly refers to his "official duty") was preserving the union:

My paramount object in this struggle is to save the union, and is not either to save or destroy slavery. If I could save the union without freeing any slave I would do it, and if I could save it by freeing all slaves I would do it; and if I could save by freeing some and leaving others alone I would also do that. What I do about slavery, and colored race, I do because I do not believe it would help to save the union…I have here stated my purpose according to my view of official duty; I and I intend to modification of my oft-expressed personal wish that all men everywhere could be free.[5]

Lincoln's comment on the singing of the proclamation was: "I never, in my life, felt more certain that I was doing right, than I do in signing this paper"[6]

On 15th April 1865 good Friday Lincoln was assassinated by John Wilkes Booth at ford theatre. Lincoln dead but his self confidence, courage, and determination is being celebrated not just in United States but all over the world. I don't know what the world would have looked like today if this man did not take such a bold step? I believe, Lincoln self confidence gave birth to Martin Luther King Jr.

> *Where they gave birth to you is not important as to where you are giving birth your dreams yourself belief will determine that, whether its maternity determination, or procrastination is up to you, any of the wards are free for you.*

American civil rights leader. In his tombstone the inscription reads, "Free at last. Free at last. Thank God almighty I'm free at last." The quote is from a religious or spiritual folk song, which King often used to close his speeches. King was killed in 1968, but his words and philosophy continue to inspire many in the United States and around the world. I also believe, if not for that emancipation of slaves the world may not have seen the first black American president Barak Obama. Friend, men that have confidence in their dream can die but they don't go to the grave with their dreams, it will always out leave them Leadership among other things, self confidence is a solid rock with which other qualities of leadership can stand and without self confidence followers will not be confident of your principles and leadership. You have to build confidence if your followers will have confident in you.

Any product you are carrying if you don't have confidence in the product it will be hard for you to convince someone about it, that is how it is in leadership. They believe your product (potentials) which helps you believe yourself that is what helps others believe in you. Friend, where they gave birth to you is not important what is important is where are you giving birth your dreams yourself belief will determine that, whether its maternity determination, or procrastination is up to you any of the wards are free for you.

Focus

Mary Kay Ash is the founder and chairwoman of highly esteemed cosmetics company Mary Kay Cosmetics. This company has become a global phenomenon, today in any leading cosmetics shop in the world Mary Kay is ranked among the best if not the best.

But had many issues that would have made her become defocus but this unique trait made her not just celebrity but an icon to her world. Her focus in life made the world to focus on her products.

This was a woman that started taking care of her father who was bedridden with tuberculosis at very tender age before the age of ten. She got divorced by her first husband that made her to drop out of premed courses she was taking at the University of Houston she went into odd jobs to see to the up bringing of her children. Her second husband collapsed with heart attack. Her third husband, Mel Ash, a retiring manufacturing representative, died in 1980 after 14 years of marriage.

Her 25 years life savings she made in a male corporate world was $5,000. She gambled this money and launched Mary Kay Cosmetics a gamble that paid off heavily.

Challenges are gifts that force us to search for a new center of gravity. Don't fight them. Just find a new way to stand.

Friend, unique leaders are men and women that are focused on their strengths and needs all around them in connection to themselves and especially the needs of others. In that way they are impacting lives around them. The whole essence of leadership is to become a solution to people around you.

Focused leaders are not distracted by the circumstances of things around them but they are made bold with circumstances because is the ladder they use to climb the next stage of success. Focused leaders see life as a stage to display their unique qualities that makes them unique.

She is what William James (1902) Harvard Psychologist called twice born. She, according to Zaleznik (1977) who commented on the twice born concept, "grew through mastering painful conflict during the developmental years. Leaders are twice born individuals who endure major events and crises that lead to a sense of separateness and estrangement from their environment." In her own case the twice born scenario came from her childhood and important relationships with people close to her. Instead of being disturbed by these experiences, never to recover, Mary Kay mastered her personal tragedies which is focus.

Oprah Winfrey asserted "Challenges are gifts that force us to search for a new center of gravity. Don't fight them. Just find a new way to stand." Unique Leaders are focused on the major tasks, roles and priorities at all times no matter how much challenges that is confronting them. To avoid casualty don't approach life casually. If you approach life casually life has a way of giving you casual results.

The best thing you should do for yourself and your organization is to focus on your call don't try to do what everybody is doing, lost of focus is lost of your glorious destination in life. You should also understand that the speed of the leadership is what determines that speed of the organization.

Staying power, character

Character in leadership is not negotiable it is the staying power that sustains you and your organization solidly. You don't enjoy uniqueness in leadership when you are having a character crisis. Character is not a word we speak during leadership seminars but a life we live both in secret and in open. Unique leaders understand the importance of character, having talent, skills, gifts, even potentials are wonderful but without character you have no foundation. Character is among the foundation that holds leadership. Johann Wolfgang von Goethe remarks "Talent develops in quiet places, character in the full current of human life."

> *The greatest threat to your leadership is not lack of resources, equipments, training, authorities, money, No, but lack of character.*

Without good character there is nothing unique about your leadership. Character! Character!! It is the engine that keeps you flying in leadership without being afraid of any failure; it is what makes you unique and distinguishes you in leadership. Friend, without character your success is limited in leadership. No limitation like limitation of character.

The greatest threat to your leadership is not lack of resources, equipments, training, authorities, money, No, but lack of character.

Dr. Hwang Woo Suk: his growing up was very rough but he has an incredible success story in quote. The son of a widow, he worked his way through school, because of lack of money he will farm for people to raise money for his tuition fees and up keeping, He grew up in a mountain town in South Korea. After his bacholor's degree he earned his doctorate in veterinary medicine, few years practicing as a veterinary doctor he entered the field of scientific research.

This man grew from nothing to something, his drive to make mark carried him all the way to a professorship at Seoul National University this was were he first got attention in the scientific community.

1999 he became a national celebrity when he announced that he has succeeded in cloning a dairy cow.

2004 he became a global celebrity when he announced that he has succeeded in creating human embryonic stem cells through cloning.

This man became very popular and influential in the medical field he was rated in the annual list of "People Who Matters" in a special issue of *Time magazine* 2004. This was a brief article posted;

A veterinarian by training, Hwang began to research cloning for a practical purpose: he wanted to create a better cow. But his work didn't stop in the barnyard. Hwang and his team at Seoul National University became the first to clone human embryos capable of yielding viable stem cells that might one day cure countless diseases. While such research raise troubling ethical questions, Hwang has already proved that human cloning is no longer science fiction, but a fact of life.[7]

2005 he was already becoming an icon in the scientific world when he announced he has successfully cloned a dog- an Afghan hound he named Snupy. At the later end of the year one of his aids came out and announced that he had ceased his collaboration with Dr. Hwang soon after another of his associate Roh Sung-IL ceased to work with him on the ground of breach of ethical conduct. He admitted that he used to pay women to donate their eggs, that were used in Hwang research.

At first he denied of everything that was said against him. When the heat became much he resigned from all his official post He also apologized for his actions. In the interview he said, *"I was blinded by work and my drive for achievement."* He denied coercing his researchers into donating eggs and claimed that he found out about the situation only after it had occurred."[8]

Leading without character is like swimming across the ocean without life jackets

He added that he had lied about the source of the eggs donated to protect the privacy of his female researchers, and that he was not aware of the Declaration of Helsinki which clearly enumerates his actions as a breach of ethical conduct."[9]

Snupy dog is the only thing him and his team cloned and they are they first in the world to clone Dog but the rest are all lies. Dr. Hwang got potential but he lacks character. Friend hear this, leading without character is like swimming across the ocean without life jacket. Living without character is like building without a foundation. Character is the staying power of any powerful leader you see today in the world both past and present. Leadership is meaningless without a meaningful conscious work of character.

This was a man that has become a national hero they created a postage stamp in his honor, have received several awards, he received millions of money people were donating for his work. Friend, if you miss the place of character in leadership you have missed the place of envy and honor in leadership. Men of character are men of strong ethical values. Nothing makes you unique in leadership when you have character; nothing makes you look stupid in leadership when you lack character. You become an idol in leadership when you have a staying power in character.

Teamwork

Leaders who demonstrate unique abilities with a touch of persistence, tenacity, enthusiasm, determination, and synergistic communication skills will bring out the same qualities in their groups. Coach Dean Smith advised Michael Jordan in his fresh year at UNC "Michael if you can't pass, you can't play" he was simply instructing him that his talent alone can't give him the desired success, he needs to work as a team to win games later in his carrier when Michael understood the power of teamwork he asserted "Talent wins the games, but teamwork and intelligence wins championships"[10] Ken Blanchard remarks "None of us is as smart as all of us" friend, there is nothing like "I" in teamwork. What makes a leader unique is in his ability to unites and bring his followers to work as a team to achieve organizational success not as an individual.

According to the National School Boards Association (USA)

These Group Leadership or Leadership Teams have specific characteristics:

Characteristics of a Team

➤ There must be an awareness of unity on the part of all its members.

➤ There must be interpersonal relationship. Members must have a chance to contribute, learn from and work with others.

➤ The member must have the ability to act together toward a common goal.

Ten characteristics of well-functioning teams:

➤ Purpose: Members proudly share a sense of why the team exists and are invested in accomplishing its mission and goals.

- Priorities: Members know what needs to be done next, by whom, and by when to achieve team goals.

- Roles: Members know their roles in getting tasks done and when to allow a more skillful member to do a certain task.

- Decisions: Authority and decision-making lines are clearly understood.

- Conflict: Conflict is dealt with openly and is considered important to decision-making and personal growth.

- Personal traits: members feel their unique personalities are appreciated and well utilized.

- Norms: Group norms for working together are set and seen as standards for everyone in the groups.

- Effectiveness: Members find team meetings efficient and productive and look forward to this time together.

- Success: Members know clearly when the team has met with success and share in this equally and proudly.

- Training: Opportunities for feedback and updating skills are provided and taken advantage of by team members.

CHAPTER FIVE

EXCELLENT LEADERSHIP

There is this believe that excellent leadership is something that comes with some few personalities by birth, others are of the view that these leadership characteristic and traits are packaged as part of their DNA cosmetics. They are born with the gift for excellent leadership. Wow!

But it might interest you to note that excellent leaders are not born with it but rather they are nurtured and inspired into excellent that has made them to become an Excellencies in their field of specialization.

Vince Lombardi asserted "Leaders aren't born they are made. And they are made just like anything else, through hard work. And that's the price we'll have to pay to achieve that goal, or any goal."

What you nurtured will soon mature into what you desire. The must important thing now is not that you desired to have an excellent leadership but you should work to have an excellent leadership it does not start from the surface but it begins with the inner man which is your spirit. Lawrence M. Miller remarks "Excellence is not an accomplishment. It is a spirit, a never-ending process."

Friend you don't excel in leadership when you not developed an excellent spirit which result into an excellent leadership

Television legend

If you call her a screen goddess, the most celebrated woman of 20th century, an icon, the most influential woman in the world, the most celebrated talk show host on the earth, you will still be referring to the same person, Oprah Winfrey. Forbes named her the world's most powerful celebrity in 2005, 2007, 2008 and 2010. Through the power of media, the name Oprah has grown beyond being a global brand into a religion of some sort, millions of followers across the world.

In 1993, she hosted a rare prime time interview with Michael Jackson, which turned out to be the fourth most watched event in American television history also the most watched interview ever, with an audience of 36.5 million."[1]

Life magazine named Oprah one of the 100 people who changed the world, along such luminaries as Jesus Christ, Elvis Presley and Lady Mary Wortley Montagu. She was the only living to make the list."[2]

In 2008 she endorsed presidential candidate then, Barack Obama, she held fundraiser for Obama on September 8, 2007, at her Santa Barbara estate. It was believed to be one of the vital forces that gave birth the first ever African-American president of United States of America.

All these and more that made this woman who she is did not come with her from birth except her potentials. Her beginning looked so messed up, blank without hope of a better tomorrow.

Before the stardom

Vernita Lee a single teenager from Kosciusko, Mississippi gave birth to Oprah Winfrey on January 29, 1954. Her mother was a housemaid, while his father Vernon Winfrey was into many odd jobs to earn himself a living such as coal miner, barber, city council man etc.

Vernita Lee left Winfrey after birth traveled north, the responsibility of her up bringing was saddled on her grandmother Hattie Mae Lee, and Oprah spent her six year living in rural poverty with her grandma. Hattie Mae Lee was so poor that Oprah often wore dresses made of potato sacks, for which the local children made fun of her."3

> *You don't excel in leadership when you not developed an excellent spirit which result into an excellent leadership*

She was so poor that even the poor people around her call her "poor girl." She says her poverty was constantly rubbed in her face as she rode the bus to school with fellow African-Americans, some of whom were servants of her classmates' families. She began to steal money from her mother in an effort to keep up with her free-spending peers to lie and argue with her mother, and to go out with older boys."4

At age two-and-half Hattie Mae Lee, taught her how to read and write.

At age six she moved in with her mother Vernita, who was a maid, she could not take up the responsibility of Winfrey because of other responsibilities she was saddled with she sent her to be with her father Mr. Vernon temporarily, when she came back her mum Vernita has given birth to a son named Jeffery.

At thirteen after suffering years of abuse, she ran away from home.

At age fourteen she became pregnant and gave birth to a son who died at infancy age. Her frustrated mother sent her to be with the father again, though this time she didn't bother to take her back again.

Vernon made her education a topmost priority, he made her read at least one book a week and to write a report on the book. She was also to memories five new words each day. She became an honor student, was voted most popular girl, and joined her high school speech team at East Nashville High school. She also won an oratory contest which **You don't become your wish you only become you believe.** secured her admission and full scholarship to Tennessee State University where she studied communication.

At age seventeen, she won the Miss Black Tennessee beauty pageant.

Despite all odd she passed through, she was determined by the help of grandma, and her father to pursue excellent in all she does. In one of the interview she was asked from a troubled teen, she rose to her statues as one of the most powerful women in television. Her answer was that "she made a commitment to pursue excellent in everything she did" all these failures where very evident all around her but was far away inside her I believe. True excellence starts from the inner to the outer. It is a conscious determination to pursue and give a touch of excellent in everything thing one does not minding the circumstance that surrounds you as a leader. Excellent leader don't look around them but they look within them and brings out the doggedness of excellent leadership while their followers look up to them to draw inspiration to become an excellent leaders. Friend hear this, you don't become your wish you only become you believe. So whatever challenge you are passing through now is only but a test to your excellent leadership. Oprah Winfrey once said, "Challenge is gifts that force us to search for a new center of gravity. Don't fight them. Just fined a new way to stand"

Tomorrow to me is only but a normal phrase of lazy men. Any result of tomorrow is simply a work of today.

Impact of hard work.

Hard work in relation to your potential, talent, gifts pays heavily. Many don't realize the impact they can make with their potential that is much reason while few have left their potential very dormant in pursuit of credentials. Friend, your potential is far greater then your credentials, until you lay hold of your potential you will never command maximum influence. Your ability to lay hold at it makes you influential in your world. Friend, getting hold of your potential makes you a global influence inability to lay hold at it makes you nothing but a local influence.

Your credential should be inline to your potential if you most essentially make positive impact in your leadership. Come to think of it, what would have happened if Oprah Winfrey went to study either engineering, or any other things well, you and I know may be she would not have gotten this far. But she pursues excellent inline to her potential coupled with hard work. It is hard work that will deliver you from hard life and is not just working hard but working SMART.

Excellent leaders don't believe the promises of tomorrow.

Until you take step today nothing steps into your tomorrow.

Excellent leaders don't believe the promises of tomorrow but a conscious believe of what they can do today that will help them live tomorrow. Friend, tomorrow to me is only but a normal phrase of lazy men. Any result of tomorrow is simply a work of today.

I love this Chinese proverb "he who deliberates fully before taking a step will spend his entire life on one leg. Until you take step today nothing steps into your tomorrow.

Edger Guest wrote a poem that explain this issue very well, it is titled *"To-morrow"*

Value System of Leadership

He was going to be all that a mortal should be

To-morrow

No one should be kinder or braver than he

To-morrow

A friend who was troubled and weary he knew,

Who'd be glad of a lift and who needed it, too,

On him he would call and see what he could do

To-morrow

Each morning he stacked up the letters he'd write

To-morrow

It was too bad; indeed, he was busy to-day,

And hadn't a minute to stop on his way;

More time he would have to give others, he'd say

To-morrow

The greatest of workers this man would have been

To-morrow

The world would have known him, had he ever seen

To-morrow

But the fact is he died and he faded from view,

Was a mountain of things he intended to do

To-morrow₅

Tomorrow is meaningless without a meaningful and diligent work of today. And your level of diligent today to your purpose is what determines your level of delegates you will hang with tomorrow. Excellent leaders have discovered that is only the light of today that will sustain you tomorrow. Stop waiting for tomorrow that never come it is what you do today that will determine where and what you will be tomorrow.

Personal Qualities of Excellent Leader

Any leadership that desires excellent leadership most imbibe few of these qualities in his or her personal life to enjoy absolute influence in your field of endeavors, there are;

Excellent leaders have an Exemplary Character.

Character and leadership is two inseparable Siamese twin. When a leader has character problem definitely he will have leadership problem. Excellent Leadership demands that you   (leader) becomes a role models for them (*followers*). The leadership should be the standard for moral living;

Character and leadership is two inseparable Siamese twin.

I have said it that living by

example makes you a sample for your followers. Any standard you set in your organization will determine how you will standout or stranded watch it.

Friend, the character you sample will determine how simple or difficulty you may encounter in your organization. Excellent leaders don't filter in their integrity, character, trust in pursuit of excellent leadership.

Excellent Leaders are Enthusiastic

Followers will naturally follow a leader that is passionately interested in what he or she does. Also followers will naturally follow a leader that has passionately followed his vision. People followed Hitler not because he was a great leader but he was so enthusiastic, passionate about his vision.

Friend, Followers don't want to know the worth of your vision until they see how you are willing and ready to die for it. Excellent leaders are enthusiastic about their work and passionate on how they will give their work and position a touch of excellent in everything they do. Excellent leaders are the source of unending inspiration to their followers.

Excellent Leaders are Confident.

When a leader lacks confidence he loses the confidence of his followers. Nothing destroys confidence as inadequate ability to set direction for your followers. Excellent leaders are confident in their ability to lead and set direction in the organization they are heading. Excellent leaders are idols whose followers draw inspiration from so they inspire confidence in their follower to accomplish great task in an uncommon way.

Excellent leaders set Direction

Excellent leaders understand uncertainty very well that makes them calm when face to face with challenges, they are composed and steadfast to the actual purpose because they understand and knows the actual destination.

They believe that challenges, difficulties, crisis are pot- hole to their journey which they most encounter if they most excel. They understand that any leadership without a defined direction will only end you nowhere but doom

Excellent Leaders set Goals

Friend, when you don't set goals in life you will end like a goat. You will agree with me that in soccer they have a goal post so without a goal post you cannot score a goal that is how it is in

I believe the choice to be excellent begins with aligning your thoughts and words with the intention to require more from yourself.

leadership without a definite goal you can't make progress in your pursuit of Excellent leadership.

Excellent leaders understand the importance of goal and not only do they view it as a whole but able to break it into subs mini, micros, minor, and major goals for closer assessment which makes it manageable

Excellent leaders are committed to Excellence.

Vincent T. Lombardi asserted "The quality of a person's life is in direct proportion to their commitment to excellence, regardless of their chosen field of endeavor." excellent leaders are men and women that is committed to excellence, they do not compromise values or standards.

Excellent leadership is not a gift but a choice one makes to become an excellent leader in his personal endeavor Oprah Winfrey observed "I believe the choice to be excellent begins with aligning your thoughts and words with the intention to require more from yourself."

This personal uniqueness is foundational to excellent leadership. Some uniqueness may be more naturally present in the behavior of a leader. Though, each of this uniqueness can also be developed and strengthened. Excellent leaders whether they naturally possess these qualities or not, will be careful to constantly develop and strengthen it.

Leadership Principles of excellent leadership

The following is a list of important principles listed at *Path to Extraordinary Leadership* posted on October 26, 2008. All these are reflective in their daily activities both in decision making and action taking.

Strong Not Rude

An Extraordinary Leader is strong, assertive and decisive, while at the same time being respectful and courteous when dealing with others.

Kind Not Weak

An Extraordinary Leader shows a gentle kindness when the situation requires. However, it would take a fool to assume that this kindness is a sign of weakness. The kindness shown by an Extraordinary Leader is rather a sign of respect for those he/she deals with on a daily basis.

Bold Not a Bully

An Extraordinary Leader takes massive fearless action and does whatever is required to get the job done. However, this does not mean that they bully their way towards their goals and objectives. Instead they progressively navigate and persuade their way through people and obstacles towards their desired outcomes.

Thoughtful Not Lazy

An Extraordinary Leader takes time to think and ponder their leadership style and circumstances each and every day in order to improve the outcomes they desire to bring forth into their life.

This should not be mistaken as laziness.

Proud Not Arrogant

An Extraordinary Leader is proud of their work, their people and their accomplishments. Yet you will not hear them bragging about their achievements to others.

Humble Not Timid

An Extraordinary Leader is humble about their accomplishments and abilities. They rather give credit to others than take it for themselves. This should not be mistaken for timidness which stems from a lack of confidence in one's abilities.

Witty Not Silly

An Extraordinary Leader is witty in nature. They are cunning and clever in their approach to people, events and circumstances.[6]

Strong pillars of excellent leadership

If you desire to be an excellent leader in any field of endeavor you must abed by these pillars. Excellence is not a word we say but is an act we choose to live with. Few of these pillars will help you that life but it all depends on you.

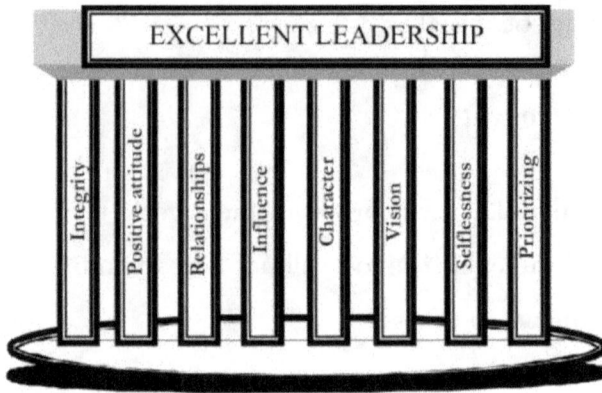

Integrity

There is no excellence in leadership when there is absence of Integrity. Integrity is the alignment between our words and action. The credibility of your leadership is determined by your ability to display a sense of integrity both in words and character. When integrity is lacking excellence is missing in leadership. Excellent leaders are builders of in integrity both in word and action.

Friend, you don't become a distinguish leader when you have not distinguish yourself in your integrity. Followers are not moved by words you say but they are moved by the action that accompanies your words. You excel in leadership when you have distinctively excelled in your integrity.

Excellent leaders are positively minded individuals with a doggedness of positive attitude.

Positive attitude

Attitude is what determines success or failure in leadership. Excellent leaders don't underestimate the power of positive attitude in leadership. Former Prime minister of England Winston Churchill said, "Attitude is a small thing that makes the huge distinction." Friend, attitude is what determines your destination and distinction in leadership. Excellent leaders are advocate of positive attitude not just in words but in character.

Excellent leaders are positively minded individuals with a doggedness of positive attitude. More of this is extensively discussed in chapter two.

Relationships

Excellent leaders understand the power of relationship that is while they take their time to treasure every relationship that comes their way. They know that relationships are the most valuable and essential asset in building excellent leadership.

Friend, creating excellent relationship with your people creates excellent environment in your organization in doing this, you most earn their respect, and trust. Ralph Waldo Emerson wrote, "the glory of friendship is not in the outstretched hand, nor the kindly smile, nor the joy of companionship; it is in the spiritual inspiration that comes to one when he discovers that someone else believes in him and is willing to trust him." Any solid relationship is built on solid trust. Excellent leaders understand the importance of leadership trust very well so they make sure that everything around them is centered on trust. If your followers cannot trust you they cannot entrust their destiny into your hand.

Influence

Kenneth Blanchard observed "The key to successful leadership today is influence, not authority." Any man you cannot inspire you cannot influence. Excellent leadership is the ability to inspire your followers to be the best they are capable of becoming.

Friend, when you inspire people, they allow you to influence them. Inspiration causes influence while influence produces leadership. James C. Georges of the Per-training Corporation asked clearly in an interview with Executive Communications: "What is leadership? Remove for a moment the moral issues behind it, and there is only one definition: Leadership is the ability to obtain followers" obtaining followers is in your ability to inspire them which produce influence and without influence there is no leadership.

Character

The former US General, Norman H. Schwarzkopf said, "Nineteen nine percent of leadership failures are character failures." Friend hear this; if you fail in the location of character

Character is the gate way to excellent leadership.

the allocation of your possession in pursuit of excellent leadership will fail you. When a leader's character increase positively his favor level increases. Nothing terminates destiny like character flaws.

Excellent leaders have developed an excellent character which reflects into excellent organization. Where the place of character is missing the place of leadership is obviously missing. Norman Schwarzkopf remarks "Leadership is a potent combination of strategy and character. But if you must be without one, be without the strategy." Character is the gate way to excellent leadership.

Vision

Excellent leadership is futile without vision. Vision is the inners eye that sees the reality before it becomes obvious. "Without vision the people perish" what avert failure in leadership is ability to conceive a vision which gives you a sense of direction, a sense of purpose, a sense of focus and a sense of objective. Friend, visionless leadership is nothing but a dead leadership.

Excellent leaders understand the route and know how to take their follower through the route. They have a clear vision for the organization they are leading. What makes excellent leaders unique is the ability to communicate the vision to their followers. Vision is a dynamic factor that makes a unique difference in leadership.

Vision help you see beyond your natural eye can see it is what gives the carrier of the vision a burning enthusiasm, passion, commitment and determination to achieve outstanding results in his or her individual field of Endeavour.

Selflessness

Selflessness is an act of coming out of your shelf of selfishness that is what makes you an excellent leader. Each and every one of us is selfish in nature but ability to come out of that shelf of selfishness makes us a leader. Most time our interest intends to becloud the interest of the organization but is in the ability of our selflessness to put the interest of the organization above our own for the good of the organization and teamwork.

Friend, leadership is ability to set aside one's selfish interest, wishes, desire for the good and benefit of the organization. Wow! You don't become a selfless leader when you have not worked on your selfishness.

Prioritizing

Excellent leaders understand the nitty-gritty of prioritizing their work. They are not time wasters they understand that every wasted time is a wasted destiny. Setting priority helps you maximize your time in every area of your life while inability to do that procrastination becomes your closest neighbor.

Procrastination will show you the time table but never allows you to fulfil it.

Friend, Procrastination will show you the time table but never allows you to fulfill it; excellent leaders know how to turn procrastination into urgency.

Setting priorities helps you set your life. Any life that lacks priority lacks a clear vision of its destination.

If you need an excellent leadership you should learn how to priorities because prioritizing is the test of excellent leadership. As you make excellent your greatest task you will become an internal excellence to your generation.

Jon Johnston professor of sociology Pepperdine University makes this dissimilarity between more success and excellence:

*Success bases our worth on a comparison with others. Excellent gauges our value by measuring us against our own potential. Success grants its rewards to the few but is the dream of the multitudes. Excellent is available to all living beings but is accepted by the... few. Success focuses its attention on the external – becoming the beams its spotlight on the internal spirit... excellence cultivates principles and consistency.*₇

As you make it a duty to pursue excellence inline to your values, your life and organization will never remain the same but still remember that excellent is not a gift is a choice you make. In that way you should be careful of people you choice to be your friend. Friend hear this; your friends are the thermometers of your destiny watch it.

CONCLUSION

Nelson Mandela stated "It is better to lead from behind and to put others in front, especially when you celebrate victory, when nice things occur. You take the front line when there is danger. Then people will appreciate your leadership." Taking organizational blame makes you exceptional leader. Giving the credit to your followers when there is a millstone achievement makes you a wonderful leader. But ironically is a different tune in my continent. Africa is where some so called "leaders" takes the victory and blames their followers for the short comings but today change is coming speedily. Despite all these, friend:

I see a land that flows with milk and honey

I see land where the natural inhabitant

Will be free of wants

I see a land where the rest of the world

Will be seeking for greener pasture

I see a land that will feed the rest of the world

I see a land that is rich in natural mineral resource

I see a land that is full of potentials, gifts, and talents,

I see a land where people will work with their

Potential not with their credentials

I see a land where true leadership will be practice

I see a land where men and women will be lovers of

Themselves not lovers of money

I see a land that will one day rule the world

Yes, I see a land! I see a land!!

…That land is Africa!

Am not saying this because am an African, or

Black but because am a citizen of the world

I can see the watch ticking yes, I can see it!

If you can see it with me the whole world will

See it with us.

Friend, God created each and everyone us in a unique manner and in each continents of the world to fulfill purpose. Friend, don't seek to be known seek to know soon the world will start seeking after you. But it has to start with

> *Taking organizational blame makes you exceptional leader. Giving the credit to your followers when there is a millstone achievement makes*

understanding of your values that makes you who you really are. The truth is you are not in this world to make up the numbers but you are here to fulfill purpose. Everything you do you should be conscious of the purpose of God for your life. When you discover your worth in life your value changes that is what this book is all about, helping you to discover and rediscover your real abilities

Please make it a point to apply the lessons, principles, information's and stories you got from this book because nothing works if you don't make it to work. I sincerely appreciate you for finding time to go through this book I believe your life and organization will definitely take a new look. I hank you once more.

NOTE

CHAPTER 1

1. http://myblogcatchup.blogspot.com/2010/06/visionary-leader-that-africa-has.html accessed 26th February 2011.

2. John C. Maxwell, 360 degree leader (Nashville: Thomas Nelson 2005), 79

3. Quoted in john wooden with Steve Johnson, author unknown, wooden: A lifetime of hat observations and reflections on and off the court (Chicago: contemporary books 1997)

4. http://www.canadaone.com/ezine/may99/leadership6.html accessed 28th February 2011.

CHAPTER 2

1. http://www.juran.com accessed on 16th July 2011

2. The 21 irrefutable laws of leadership (C) 1998 and 2007 by John C. Maxwell), 186

3. http://www.agiftofinspiration.com.au/stories-at-authorunknown accessed on 15th July 2011

CHAPTER 3

1. http://www.customerservicepoint.com/loyalty-quotes.html) accessed 24th July 2011

CHAPTER 4

1. http://www.manifestyourpotential.com/self-dis. through mobile phone accessed 22rd September 2011

2. http://www.winston-church-leadership.com/tr, through mobile phone accessed 23rd September 2011

3. Donald(1996) pp 364-365)

4. James M. McPherson, Abraham Lincoln and the second American Revolution (Oxford UP., 1992) 142.

5. Donald (1996) p. 368

6. Ibid.

7. http://www.time.com/time/asia/2004/personoftheyear/people/hwang-woo-suk.html, accessed 27th September 2011

8. http://en.wikipedia.org/wiki/Hwang-suk, accessed 18th November 2011

9. Ibid.

10. http://www.leadership-tools-com/team-building, accessed 24th September 2011

CHAPTER 5

1. Company, Johnson Publishing (March 8, 1993) "Alex Haley's 'Queen' Lifts CBS TO NO1 Jet magazine 37

2. Life Magazine: 100 people who changed the world. August 20th, 2010

3. "You go girl" "the observer profile: Oprah Winfrey. The observer (UK), November 20th , 2005

4. Nagle, Jeanne M. *Oprah Winfrey: Profile of a Media Mogul* Rosen Publishing, 2007), 12.

5. Edger A. Guest, "To-morrow," A heap O' Livin'(Chicago: Reilly and Lee, 1916)

6. Path to extraordinary leadership posted October 26th, 2008. www.path-to-extraordinary-leadership-mind-map.htm, accessed December 2rd. 2011

7. Jon Johnston, Christian Excellence (Grand Rapids: Baker Book House, 1985), 30.

ABOUT THE BOOK

This book will bring back your self-worth! It is a highly motivational, inspiring, and above all spiritual masterpiece that will change your life forever. This masterpiece will enable you to lead your life and empower others.

The Value System of Leadership will fill your life with what it takes to become a creative force and a force to reckon with.

- ❖ It will empower you to become what you are created to be.
- ❖ It will teach you lessons that will help you rediscover yourself.
- ❖ It will build your self-esteem, values and enhance your self-worth.
- ❖ It will give you the necessary tools you need to locate eternally assigned destinies and fulfil your purpose for living.

It does not matter how long you have been seeking to lead, live and work with the right understanding of who you truly are. It does not matter how people have assessed you in the time past. The Value System of Leadership will open your eyes to understand and get wise to life-changing principles of Leadership that will enable you to make power-choices that will empower many, increase your influence, enhance your value creation and inspire transformation that delivers the future.

W isdom K. Ogbuagu is the President of Wiskele Nets Ltd. He is a highly principled, disciplined man who lives by the strength of his convictions.

Among the end-time apostolic gifts to the body of Christ, he is a strong and forthright preacher, teacher of the Word, motivational speaker, a mentor and father to those God has placed under his ministry. He has so much insight in wisdom, purpose, developing friendships, leadership and understanding the person of the Holy Spirit.

A prolific writer and anointed preacher, and pastor who is dedicated to making sure his gifts and wealth of experience are edifying to the body of Christ and the secular world at large, a harvest that will impact future generations. He is happily married to Mrs. Comfort O. Wisdom

www.ingramcontent.com/pod-product-compliance
Lightning Source LLC
LaVergne TN
LVHW051749080426
835511LV00018B/3276